W9-DJN-627

Youth
At
Bat

Youth
At
Bat

Chester E. Swor and Jerry Merriman

WITHDRAWN
by Unity Library

Fleming H. Revell Company
Westwood, New Jersey

UNITY SCHOOL LIBRARY
Unity Village
Lee's Summit, Missouri 64063

The Scripture quotations in this publication are taken from the *King James Version of the Bible,* unless otherwise identified.

The Scripture passages identified as PHILLIPS in this publication are from *The New Testament in Modern English,* translated by J. B. Phillips. Copyright © by J. B. Phillips. Used by permission of the Macmillan Company.

COPYRIGHT © 1968 BY FLEMING H. REVELL COMPANY · ALL RIGHTS RESERVED · WESTWOOD, NEW JERSEY · LIBRARY OF CONGRESS CATALOG CARD NUMBER 68-17095 · PRINTED IN THE UNITED STATES OF AMERICA · 1.1

BV
531.2
59

Dedication

To Mr. and Mrs. Frank L. Fair, beloved friends of the authors of this book, and long time and devoted friends of young people.

The vital interest and tangible support given by Mr. and Mrs. Fair to the authors of this book in their widening contacts with high schools through the Character Emphasis Week approach have been an investment in the one great treasure of our nation with which nothing else can compare—*the character strength of today's young people, tomorrow's leaders.*

For the many thousands of young people who, the authors hope, will glean strength from the pages of this little book, we say to Mr. and Mrs. Fair, "Thank you so much for caring enough to make possible an additional source of strength for those of us who face today's youth battles with hope of victory for today and for tomorrow!"

Introduction

I am glad to see a book like *Youth at Bat.*

With the many adjectives available in the English language, that may sound like faint praise, but I assure you it is not. It is like a man who, upon receiving an award, faces the audience and merely says, "Thank you." There's more sincerity and meaning in those simple words than in all the planned words he could prepare— and that is the way I feel about *Youth at Bat.*

As a baseball player, I know the problems Chester E. Swor and Jerry Merriman had to overcome in writing a book which attempts to portray Biblical personages and events in baseball terms. In my opinion, they've done it brilliantly, drawing many parallels between the Bible and baseball that cannot help but make *Youth at Bat* one of the most interesting and rewarding books active, sports-minded young people can read. Anyone who considers religion "dull" is in for a big surprise when he reads *Youth at Bat,* I promise you.

Most important, of course, is that youth really is at bat in the game of life. Each young person has the same opportunity as his fellow players to strike out or hit safely, and this analogy to baseball is sound and remarkably accurate. There is a clear parallel, for example, between David facing Goliath and a new, untried ballplayer in the batter's box, staring into the eyes of a major league pitcher for the first time. It's a time of tension, calling for courage, coolness and a large helping of faith and confidence. As it was with David, so it is with the ballplayer: The opposing pitcher and team are doing their best to retire him from the field, and so are about half of the fans. The player who comes through is the one with something "special" inside of him. That something "special" is what *Youth at Bat* is all about.

Jonah faced a typical ballplayer's problem when he chose to avoid a demanding situation and do his best, regardless of the odds. He not only caused what could definitely be called an error for his team, but he struck out dramatically as far as his own immediate success was concerned. The Prodigal Son is a classic Biblical example of refusing to obey the orders of the coach, only to find out that this refusal meant complete personal failure.

INTRODUCTION

I can tell you that during my many years as the Yankee's second baseman I have seen many men whose actions and problems—successes and failures—conform remarkably to those of David, Jonah, the Prodigal Son and the many other persons and situations described in *Youth at Bat.*

Interestingly enough—and I don't think it's beside the point—I also feel that *Youth at Bat will help anyone to become a better ballplayer!* I'm not sure that's what the authors had in mind, but I am sure that the rules for success in life and sports are pretty much alike. In both cases, you have to have faith in your coach and in yourself. In both cases, you must follow the rules if you hope to measure up to your true potential, and you must *practice,* whether it's your fielding and batting ability in baseball or controlling your temper and witnessing to your faith in life.

Obviously, I could cite a much longer list of meaningful similarities, but the authors have done it for me in a much more imaginative way that will appeal to you from the first page to the last.

Doctor Swor and Mr. Merriman are dedicated to youth, and to the future of youth. In choosing to write their book in baseball terms, they are not only guaranteeing the reader an enjoyable and meaningful few hours, they are also providing me with a great privilege—that of seeing my sport, and my career, become yet another vehicle for witnessing to Christ.

As I said in the beginning, I am glad to see a book like *Youth at Bat.*

And you will be, too.

Bobby Richardson

Foreword

BATTER UP! Those two words have sent tingles of excitement and hope through players and fans alike through the decades of baseball history. The pitcher hopes to outwit the batter; the batter hopes to connect for a hit; the team and fans, though opposed in hope, are united in excitement that this will be the big inning.

Youth is "at bat" today as never before, and the issues at stake are vastly more significant than the outcome of a single baseball game. The forces that wish to capture youth's strength and potential for selfish, even destructive, uses are bidding for him as never before; and the fans on that side are more numerous and vociferous than ever. The forces which wish to steer youth to greater strength and usefulness have their hopes riding on his performance at bat, too. If he strikes out, many who love him will be disappointed, and some other young people whom he influences will probably strike out, too. If he hits and scores, his fans will rejoice, and his young friends will be encouraged.

Youth at Bat has been written to encourage young people to play the game of character well, to tell them some reasons *why*, and to suggest some ways *how*. Jerry Merriman, writer of half of these chapters, though young in years, is an old hand at baseball, having played the game with enthusiasm from the age of thirteen on through university graduation. He has been at bat scores of times on the baseball diamond, and he is still at bat as a young person making destiny-determining decisions. Dr. Chester Swor, prevented by physical limitations from being at bat on the baseball field, has been at bat with young people in decision-making for more than thirty years. He has seen some young people strike out, and he has seen many hit home runs.

In this little book, these two writers seek to share with today's young people some of the counsel which, as a team, they share in high schools, colleges, and churches throughout America. Without being slavish to the informal diction of teen-agers—"real gone" if you please—they have written informally with the hope that the reading will be easy, enjoyable, and, most of all, helpful.

So, *batter up!* It's time for *you*, young friend, to come to grips with some issues which will determine the outcome of this wonderful game of life. The two authors, both ardent friends of youth, hope with all their hearts that this little volume will help you achieve the best batting average humanly possible!

C.E.S. and J.J.M.

Contents

1

Game Time

(*Acts 24* [*particularly verse 25*])

"What time is it?" is one of the most common questions asked in the United States daily. When a person asks that question, he is usually trying to determine whether it is time to begin a task or to conclude one. In order to be able to answer the question correctly, one must know the time zone in which his questioner is located.

You know, of course, that there are four official time zones in our United States: When it is 5 P.M. in New York, it is 4 P.M. in Chicago, 3 P.M. in Denver, and 2 P.M. in San Francisco. So, you must know from what time zone your questioner is speaking before you can answer correctly his inquiry, "What time is it?"

In the matter of spiritual decisions, also, there are some time zones. And, in this vastly important area of a young person's life, the answer to the question, "What time is it?" will depend upon two factors: (1) whether or not the individual is a Christian; (2) if he is a Christian, the condition of his relationship to Christ.

First, what time is it in the life of a person who has not yet accepted Christ as Saviour? The answer is very clear: it is time *now* for that individual to give his heart to Christ in faith; for only when a person has made this important acceptance can he hope to achieve the success and happiness that God wishes for him.

The Bible points up clearly that the time for that all-important decision is *now*: ". . . behold, *now* is the accepted time; behold, *now* is the day of salvation," (II CORINTHIANS 6:2 [Author's italics]). "Jesus stood and cried, saying, If any man thirst, let him come unto me, and drink" (JOHN 7:37). "How shall we escape if we neglect so great a salvation. . . ?" (HEBREWS 2:3). Therefore, God's Word is saying urgently to those who have not given their hearts to Christ in faith that *now*, not later, is the wise time to make this supremely important decision.

Second, what time is it in the life of a young person who is already a Christian—a young person who desires to live his life according to the expectations of Jesus? Quite naturally, the answer is not the same for all Christians; for, indeed, Christians differ greatly in their individual rapport with Christ. In order to answer helpfully the question, "What time is it?", these possibilities must be considered:

1) For some Christians, it is time to pause to take stock of their lives—to discover whether or not they are growing as Christians ought to grow in Bible study, prayer, faith, conviction, courage and witnessing. The wise Christian will take an inventory of his life at regular intervals to make sure that his growth in these facets of spiritual development is continuing. Upon finding hindrances to spiritual growth, he will cast them aside. In discovering new aids to spiritual growth, he will incorporate them into his life. These times of inventory will assure that the Christian's spiritual growth will not only continue, but will achieve its maximum.

2) For other Christians, it is time to seek God's will, in regard to vocation; for those who have found God's will, but have not fully accepted it, it is time to say with the hymn writer: "Wherever He Leads, I'll Go."

3) For still other Christians, it is time to come back to a closer walk with Jesus in daily living. Be-

cause these individuals have "followed Jesus afar off" in their daily living, they have lost the power and joy which come only to Christians who follow *Him* closely. How wonderful it would be for *you,* if you have been following Jesus unfaithfully in your daily living, to say with heart and lips the opening words of a well-known hymn, "All To Jesus I Surrender."

4) For some other Christians, it is time to dedicate God-given talents to fuller use in Christian service, particularly in the life of the church. All of us need to remember that the church is the bride of Christ, and that God's Word has indicated that if we do not love the bride of Christ, we do not really love Christ Himself. Two reminders may be helpful:

To the talented young person. Remember that every talent in your life is a gift from God. You do not actually own it, for God gave it to you with the expectation that you would become a good steward of that talent. Therefore, though you may have added much to that talent through study and practice, the talent itself is a gift from God, and you will not be truly grateful for it if you do not permit it to be used unselfishly in the life of your Church.

To the young person of limited talents. Remember that if you place your talents—however few or small they may be—in the hands of Christ through a total commitment of your life, He can multiply your talent-contribution as wonderfully as He multiplied the little boy's loaves and fishes, making those talents a rich blessing to many people around you. *Regardless of the quantity or quality of your abilities —small or large—are you serving as fully in your church as God has enabled you?*

5) It is time for many, many young Christians to begin to tell their non-Christian friends about Jesus. If you have been a Christian for some time, you have experienced the wonderful differences Christ makes in life. Have you shared that discovery with your friends who have not accepted Christ? If you have not shared your discoveries with non-Christian friends, isn't it logical for Christ to wonder if you really love Him—if you appreciate the transformation which He has accomplished in your life?

God has made possible our personality differences, distinctions and appeals, affording an entrée to people with whom we have rapport: you may have access to some young people whom I do not reach, while I may have entrée to some whom you do not reach. God expects us to capitalize upon these personality entrées and appeals in sharing our knowledge of Jesus with those who do not know him.

In the Scripture passage listed at the beginning of this chapter is the true-to-life episode of Paul's presentation of the message of Christ to Felix, the governor before whom he stood. Although Felix was so impressed that he trembled with conviction, he said to Paul, "Go thy way for this time; when I have a convenient season, I will call for thee." That time never came, because Felix was replaced by another governor soon thereafter.

With you, as with Governor Felix, it may be later than you think—deferring any of these important decisions on the assumption that you will have plenty of time to attend to them later may be a *presumption*. I know from my experience in life, as well as on the baseball diamond, that time runs out with amazing frequency. *What time is it with you? If it is time for you to attend to any one of the significant matters we have discussed, why not resolve that you will begin to do so now?*

What time is it? It's game time, and decision-making time is *now*. Did you hear the umpire shout, "Batter Up?" He means *you*. It's your turn at bat!

2

A Player Who Dreamed—
And Stayed Fit

(Genesis: 37)

Look who's coming up to bat, tossing his sharp-look-
ing parka of many colors into the hands of one of the
team helpers. He is Joseph, son of the Mr. Jacob,
who is smiling happily from a box in the stands.
Never liked by his buddies in his younger days because they never understood him, the victim of experiences that would have prompted many less courageous players to toss in the towel, Joseph connects
with the third pitch for a thrilling homer. And who
are those men in the stands cheering loudest for
him? The very ones who, not knowing the stuff of
which Joseph was really made, had thought him
vain, selfish, and high-hat. Dig that look of "I told
you so" on the face of the proud dad who had loved
Joseph and believed in him through the years.

Let's take a look into the background of this stellar baseball hero. His biography, as told in GENESIS 37 and subsequent chapters, is dotted in its descriptions of his growing-up days with the refrain, "And Joseph dreamed a dream. . . ." Even a casual look into the nature of the dreams reveals that they were *vocational* dreams: dreams of what he would be in his mature years if he cared, used, and developed the abilities God had given him.

Despite the villainous treatment he received from his own brothers (who, out of jealousy, sold him into slavery to an Egypt-bound caravan) and the heartbreaking imprisonment that resulted from the falsehood told about him by his employer's immoral wife, Joseph kept his own life clean; he stuck to his dream tenaciously. It is not surprising, therefore, that everything he had dreamed in his teen years, came to glorious fulfillment in his later years. Is it necessary to point out that without the dreams there would have been no fulfillment?

What about *your* dreams, as you project yourself in thought into the future? Why not forget the rest of the world for a few minutes, take an honest look into the abilities God has given you, and project yourself into the future on the wings of that lively imagination with which you are endowed? As a long-time (over three decades) coach of potential "players" I want to offer three suggestions.

First, a vocational dream is imperative if you wish to achieve anything worthwhile in the future. The news of someone's success may come suddenly; but, in all probability, the person involved had dreamed, planned, worked—even suffered—in accomplishing the unusual achievement which the world heard of suddenly. It is a part of the pattern of life all around us: develop a plan, assemble the materials, build the structure—be it building, highway, institution, or life. Without the plan, the builder does not know what materials to assemble. The very building in which you may be sitting as you read these lines was once but a dream—an architect's blueprint.

In my college days, I saw a poster with only six words on it: CHOOSERS NEVER DRIFT . . . DRIFTERS NEVER CHOOSE. If a young person has a vocational dream, he knows where he is going; he knows the preparation essential to arriving at success; he knows something of the cost involved— in money, effort and anxiety. A dream for your future is not just desirable, it is imperative, if you want your future to be significant.

When I was Dean of Men on a college campus, hundreds of wonderful young people told me of their dreams for the future. I was thrilled; I counseled with them gladly and followed their progress eagerly with interest and prayer. So many of them are now adults in positions of tremendous usefulness and influence, blessing their world.

One student shared with me his confident expectation of becoming a research chemist and of perfecting formulas that would make differences in manufacturing processes. He was only a poverty-stricken student, but he had a million-dollar dream in his heart. Through four eventful, hard-working college years he moved, through 3 more years of graduate study for a Ph. D. degree, and out into the world of chemical research. Today, he holds a position of international significance and travel with a great chemical corporation. He had his dream years ago: He has the fulfillment now!

Second, make your dream a high dream—as high as your basic abilities, adequate education, and skill-through-experience permit. Although it is not true that "you can be anything you want to be," it *is* true that you can become anything that your God-given abilities educated adequately and seasoned with experience make possible your being. In the light of those three factors, the higher you dream, the harder you will work, and the farther you will go. They laughed at Joseph for his "high dreams," but their own lives were later saved because of the fulfillment of those very dreams.

Did a junior-high-school girl dream too high, as she delivered newspapers on her bicycle in her little village? Her dream was of college, business training, and a top-level career in business. Some thought so, doubtless, because the financial depression was deep, her family had almost no funds for sending her to college, and women did not generally aspire to high-level business careers in those days. Yet, this wonderful girl kept on dreaming her dream and working toward its fulfillment. College necessitated dining-room chores, weekend work, scrimping, and sacrificing. Summertime jobs left little time for vacation.

Graduation from college came; and with it opportunity to work for a business firm in one of America's largest cities. She met a young man who had been traveling a similar path; love came joyously, and marriage ensued. They strove valiantly as marriage and business partners in a meager beginning. Progress toward success eventually accelerated, and they came to realize the success toward which they had dreamed and striven—a business enterprise with nationwide contacts. Upon the death of her husband, this "dreamer of dreams" continued heroically in the work their four hands had built; today, she is one of America's outstanding business women. What if she had dreamed a lesser dream?

Third, stick by your dream, regardless of the cost of its fulfillment. Between the time of Joseph's dreams and their fulfillment, decades elapsed— decades in which he was victimized by injustices, imprisoned, and threatened with execution. All along, he had done his work with honesty and thoroughness; even in prison, he was a useful helper to fellow-prisoners.

The fulfillment of your dream may well require many years of education—difficult and expensive years. Beyond the formal education period, there may be lean years of additional preparation and experience. Circumstances beyond your control may detour you for years from the course you had planned. You may have to sacrifice the comforts and luxuries along the way, which others of your age are enjoying. You may even have to defer marriage longer than your heart desires. And, to wax a bit Churchillian, you may be called upon to give "blood, toil, tears, and sweat," to accomplish your hopes. Yet, if the dream is worthy, the cost of fulfillment will be justified. Our Christ did not regard the frightful cost of the cross a too-high price to pay for the accomplishment of the purpose that brought him to earth—the reconciliation of man to God.

One splendid young woman was detoured for nine years beyond high school by circumstances of family need; not permitting the detour to be defeat, she entered college at twenty-seven, completed her degree at thirty-one, and is achieving superbly in her vocation. A young man, detoured by similar circumstances, entered college at twenty-seven to work toward a degree in medicine, finishing his preparation at thirty-seven. He is one of America's most successful Public Health physicians. Thousands of severely handicapped young people have amazed and inspired their friends by acquiring the finest education under almost incredible difficulties.

As he sat in my office at the outset of his freshman year, a student told me that he aspired to be one of America's outstanding surgeons—not to make money for himself, but to make available the best surgery possible for anyone who needed it, regardless of ability to pay. I asked him if he had counted the cost in the matter of years of preparation—college, medical school, internship, residency, the long hours and patient skill needed to become an outstanding surgeon. I told him that twenty-five years could well elapse before he reached the upper echelon of American surgery. With a blush of apology, lest he appear to be vain, he said with warmth and conviction, "I don't care if it takes thirty years; that's what I want to be and that's what I intend to be!"

Four years of college, four of medical school, two years of internship in those pre-World War II days, four years of residency at sixty dollars a month plus board, years of military service, years of playing second fiddle to an older surgeon followed.

Thirty years later, I was in his city for an appointment. I accompanied him to the hospital in which he performed his surgery and I saw deference I have rarely seen accorded a doctor. I heard from his friends that, during the year before, he had done thousands of dollars worth of free surgery for people who had no money. I learned that he had been accorded the highest of honors among surgeons in America.

As I left him at the end of that memorable afternoon, I was overwhelmed by the sentiment which crowded my heart. "Thirty years ago," I said to him, "you sat at my desk, told me of your dream, and said that even if its realization should take thirty years, you were completely willing to pay the cost. Here it is, thirty years, and you *are* one of America's truly great surgeons!"

Coming back to the game in which Joseph just knocked that home run, let's join the cheers of the stands with an even fuller appreciation of the batter. It is my hope that many youthful readers will want to imitate Joseph. *Dream your dream, make it a high dream, and stick by that dream to its fulfillment.* And, by the way, before you go home from the game, remember that Joseph wouldn't have been a home-run king if he had not kept fit with honesty and clean living under as hard circumstances of temptation as you will ever face!

3

He Struck Out–And How!

(*The Book of Jonah*)

Jonah knew very well what God wanted him to do, but he did not relish the assignment at all. In the light of his rebellious feelings, Jonah made two serious mistakes, errors that lost the game for him: he decided to disobey God; he thought he could run away from God and thereby escape doing the will of God. Remember his experience when he attempted to run away from God to evade doing God's will? We can be reasonably sure Jonah never forgot what happened to him! You always strike out if you disobey the will of God, and there is not the remotest chance that an individual can run away from an omnipresent God.

A rather large roster of players in the game of life have joined Jonah in this game-losing attempt to evade God's will for their lives. But, there is also a galaxy of players who have achieved wonderful success and have blessed their own and succeeding generations, because they accepted and followed God's will for their lives in the matter of vocation. Three of life's most important achievements depend upon finding and following God's will for your life.

First, maximum success depends upon doing God's will. It is not that an individual cannot achieve success at all unless he follows God's will for his life, for many have achieved what their world called success entirely outside of following God's will. Rather, it is that one cannot achieve the quality and quantity of success which God intended for his life unless he finds and follows God's will. To realize as life's innings run out that the highest significance of one's life has not been achieved is a major tragedy —all the more so in view of the "too late" dimension.

Suppose a young woman, meant for medicine, fears its exactions and goes into nursing instead. The abilities required for success as a doctor could enable her to achieve success as a nurse yet she would not be achieving God's highest purpose for her life. A young man, meant for a religious ministry, but unwilling to go into it, decides to become a teacher instead. In teaching, he can perform successfully;

but he, too, will be failing to achieve the maximum success which following God's will would have brought to him. A young person meant for *any specific vocation,* but desiring a higher level of income or comfort or prestige than that vocation offers, may achieve an excellent degree of success in *his* instead of *God's* choice of vocation; yet he will never achieve the maximum success which God had hoped for his life.

Second, fullest happiness in vocation depends upon doing God's will. As in the discussion of success, I do not mean to say that an individual will not achieve *any* happiness in vocation unless he follows God's vocational will; rather, I am saying that the superlative degree of happiness in vocation will come only to the individuals who find and follow God's will for their lives.

Have you ever wondered why missionaries, returned for furlough, glow with happiness as they speak of their work in foreign lands, often done under great difficulty and with much privation? They are supremely happy in their hearts, because they know that they are doing God's will and, therefore, have his power, companionship, and approval. In many other vocations, in which the work is hard and the compensation meager, one finds men and women whose faces and voices reveal a deep peace of heart and an overflowing joy of life. They, too, are happy, because they *know* that they are investing their lives in the game-winning principle of following God's will.

Despite the apparent happiness of those who go their own way instead of God's way to accumulate the materials to buy beauty, travel, and prestige, those who do not follow God's will do eventually reach old age; and, believe me, young friends, many of them have told me with sorrow and bitterness how they followed their stubborn plans in the face of a clear knowledge that they were disobeying God's will. In the language of baseball, they are walking off the field at game's end, ashamed to face the coach, reviewing their big error with regret, wishing to heaven they could play it all over again.

Third, making one's largest contribution to one's world depends upon following God's will in vocation. It is possible to make a contribution to your world apart from obeying God's will in vocation, but you will not be able to make the *largest* contribution to the world, which God had intended. One illustration should suffice.

Billy Graham, loved and admired and respected

by millions around the world, could have chosen to go into some other vocation than the ministry. With his magnificent personality, he could have made a large contribution to his world in any of several vocations. Yet, it is irrefutably clear, I believe, that in any other vocation he could never have made the contribution to his world that he is now making in the ministry of evangelism.

POSSIBILITY: TERRIFYING OR TREMENDOUS?

In addition to the threefold loss which will come to any individual who fails to follow God's will for his life, there is still another: one's world will suffer if he or she fails to follow God's will in vocation.

What if Florence Nightingale had not followed God's will into nursing? That distinguished profession might have been greatly delayed in developing. What if Will and Charles Mayo had not gone into medicine? We would not have the internationally known clinic that bears their name. What if Jonas Salk had not gone into medicine? We might not yet have a vaccine of that type for that once-dreaded scourge of polio. What if Winston Churchill had not gone into politics and government? The stygian blackness and the despair of the free world in the spring of 1940 might not have been lifted had it not been for his immortal words and peerless courage, which inspired fighters for freedom everywhere. *Who knows what the world might well miss if you should fail to follow God's will for your life?*

Under difficulties greater than any one of you will ever face, a young man, born in 1880, worked his way through college and medical school. There were many times he must have been tempted to turn back, but he went straight ahead with courage and dedication. At long last, his preparation was complete, and he was on his way to a little South Mississippi town to begin his medical practice.

In that little Southern town, several weeks prior to the young doctor's arrival, a six-year-old lad had been seriously injured in a playground accident. No X rays were available anywhere in that area; and though the lad was given the best attention available, he was evidently slipping into death. Upon the arrival of the magnificent young doctor, some friends sent him to the lad's home. Because of his excellent orthopedic training, he recognized the nature of the malady, performed immediate surgery, hovered over the lad with dedicated professional devotion and achieved a near-miracle in saving the boy's life.

Do you know why I am so interested in that story from the long-ago? *I was that six-year-old boy,* and would have died before my seventh birthday if that splendid man had failed to follow God's will for his life—or if he had even lost a year unnecessarily. At this writing, I have had a bit over fifty years of extra living because someone else followed God's will for his life. My gratitude for the fact that he followed God's will for his life is inexpressibly great.

For all that is involved, young friends, don't "pull a Jonah!"

4

The Squeeze Play

(I Peter 4:3, 4, 12–14 and Romans 12:2)

All of us who have played baseball understand the meaning of the expression, "squeeze play." In baseball, it is a perfectly good and right technique: sacrificing the batter's chance to score in order to get a player home from third base, for instance. In some instances, the score thus made can determine the outcome of a baseball game.

But there is another aspect to this baseball squeeze play: if alert players on the opposing team anticipate it and outwit the play, their team may well be the game's winner. In other words, the squeeze play doesn't *have* to succeed just because some players attempt it!

In the thrilling, yet hazardous game of daily living, there is another kind of squeeze play, and it doesn't *have* to succeed either. This particular squeeze play occurs in the continuing pressure of the crowd to persuade the Christian young person to "go it with the gang" regardless of where the gang is going. The crowd is not always wrong, but history proves that it has so often been wrong in destiny determining hours and issues, that it behooves the Christian to dare to discover what is right, and to stand thereupon, regardless of the opinion of the crowd.

The crowd chose Barabbas instead of Christ: concerning Christ, the crowd shouted, "Crucify him, crucify him!" The crowd thought that Columbus, Savonarola, Copernicus, Galileo, the early Roman Christians, and the Oxford martyrs were wrong: some of them suffered indignities, some, death. In our day, the crowd, as represented by the majority, often has made wrong choices at the polls. Even closer to home, the majority of a student body, or of a fraternity/sorority, or of some other student group often has decreed a basically wrong thing to be acceptable. In the light of history, the young Christian of today may well admit that a majority opinion is not always a dependable guidepost for his action choices.

Being fully aware that his fellow Christians were in a stark minority in a non-Christian society, Paul spoke a clear and unmistakable word of counsel to them in ROMANS 12:2: "Don't let the world around you squeeze you into its own mold, but let God remold your minds from within, so that you may prove in practice that the plan of God for you is good, meets all his demands and moves toward the goal of true maturity" (PHILLIPS).

According to Paul's clear challenge, the pressure upon the Christian should come from *within*, from minds that have been remolded by the infallible wisdom of God—*not* from the pressures of an unstable, self-serving crowd.

There's no need to beat around the bush or to keep this discussion from the cases in point of which you and I are aware; let's come right down to you and me and our day. Two of the greatest tests of the young Christian's willingness to stand against the crowd are met in his confrontation with *dishonesty* and *immorality,* so tragically rampant in our day.

Continuing surveys reveal that a tremendous number of high-school and college students cheat regularly and engage in other acts of dishonesty; and that the majority of dishonest students apprehended indicate no regret for what they have done. The standard rejoinder is "Well, everybody else is doing it; so, how can it be wrong?" This attitude reveals an even more tragic weakness, because it implies that honesty is a relative matter and not an absolute principle.

Another battle front for the young Christian who cares is the growing tide of sex immorality found on high-school and college campuses. As distasteful as it is to admit it, you and I who know the score must admit that a heartbreaking number of students disobey the commandment of God and the laws of man in their sex lives. In this deplorable practice, too, a widespread attempt at justification is the salient or spoken defense, "Well, practically everybody does it." This attitude has two errors: The *"practically everybody"* is false, because a tremendous number of young people are keeping God's rules of the game in this important matter and *are* waiting for marriage. This attitude seems to forget that God's commandments regarding sex chastity have been neither amended nor revoked, and that the laws of the individual states in which they live still regard sex outside of marriage as illegal.

The battle for honesty and morality will be won or lost on the basis of whether or not the young person is honest enough to stick by his convictions—convictions based upon, and documented by, God's word. The brightest star in a society darkened by dishonesty and immorality is the fact that a great number of heroic young people are refusing to let that kind of dishonest and immoral world squeeze them into its mold. Let me tell you of just a few of these young people I know.

One young man began his college life in compromise, but turned to courage and victory. During his high-school days, he had been an outstanding Christian, but, upon entering college, he ceased to live his Christianity, fearing that his crowd would not like him. During his first semester in college, he pledged a fraternity and went along with the crowd, even when the crowd went wrong. A "still small voice" within him, however, kept reminding him that the Christian is expected to be a "light of the world. . . . salt of the earth."

Admitting that he had taken the easy way with the hope of winning a popularity which is "here today and gone tomorrow," he began to decline to go with the crowd when the crowd went wrong. He began to live the kind of Christianity he once knew —the kind of Christianity which, while having the courage not to compromise, is radiant, outgoing, happy, and helpful. As a result of his return to courage, he won several of his fraternity friends to Christian faith. The entire fraternity was gradually transformed as this young man squeezed his part of his world into the Christian mold.

A young woman graduated from college and took her first job as a staff artist with an advertising firm. Not long after she had begun to work, her supervisor confronted her with a stipulation that she use her art skill in an undertaking that violated a deep Christian conviction of her life. To have complied with the stipulation (which she had understood upon accepting the position would never be made) would have amounted to using a God-given ability in an unworthy manner. Radiant in face and manner, she explained that she could not comply, and for her explanation she received a curt dismissal. Shortly thereafter, she received an offer of an even better position, but here is the finest result of her courage: the supervisor who had dismissed her from the earlier position was haunted by her radiant testimony, and he too became a Christian and an active church member.

The unwillingness of this heroic young woman makes appropriate my sharing with you two statements made long ago in a world congress of Christian young people:

"We cannot *lift* the world if we are not higher than the world."

"We cannot *move* the world if we are moved around by the world."

A survey, involving over 50,000 high-school students throughout our nation, recognized the tremendous power of "the crowd" in dictating behavior of teen-agers. It said, in essence, that some teen-agers will violate the teachings of their parents, the proscriptions of their churches, and the laws of their society rather than disagree with the crowd.

The same survey went on to say, however, that now, as in every age, there are some "White Knights" who have not succumbed to the pressures of the crowd, when the pressures were wrong. We may add without fear of contradiction that these courageous young people have not only maintained self-respect; they have often had the inner, if unspoken, respect of the crowd. Even more often, as the crowd looks back with the perspective of judgment which only years can give, it has admitted, with regret for its action, that the courageous ones were right.

In the pressure that the crowd will make upon *you* often, remember that in life, as in baseball, one could well lose the game by succumbing to the squeeze play. Remember, too, that in many glorious instances young people have won the crowd, immediately or eventually, by daring to be different when Christian convictions impelled them. Let's say it again and tuck it into our hearts for all the times we shall need it in the future: *"Don't let the world around you squeeze you into its own mold."*

(Additional reading: ROMANS 8:31.)

5

The Other Fellows
on the Team

(*Daniel: 1*)

The King of Babylon had decreed that the "cream of the crop" of young manhood of the recently transplanted captives from conquered Israel be selected, put into special training, and equipped for high-level service in the future. Among the captive Israelites chosen were Daniel and three of his buddies. When the food provisions for the trainees were announced, Daniel discovered that they contained foods not good for the body and strong drink—not good for body, mind, and spirit.

It was clear that the king took for granted that everybody drank. Practically all of the trainees accepted the food and drink provisions without complaint: "After all, isn't everybody doing it? And, if everybody is doing it, don't risk being called a square by the crowd. . . . Don't you just sort of *have to do it* if you want to get along with the crowd and influence it in the right direction? Then, too, the trainers of the various groups seem to think that you're likely to be pale, wan, and unattractive if you don't [verse 10]. So, you see, it's just easier to go along with the crowd: You don't have to explain anything; nobody will call you an 'odd pod'; and if you want to get ahead in the world, you've got to have the crowd with you!"

No such rationalizing went on in Daniel's mind: ". . . Daniel purposed in his heart that he would not defile himself with the portion of the king's meat, nor with the wine which he drank . . ." (1:8). Despite the fears of the trainer who had immediate charge of Daniel and his buddies, he permitted a ten-day trial period. At the end of the period, to his evident surprise, the trainer found that his trainees were in amazingly better physical condition than the others. Thereafter, he followed the wishes of Daniel and his group. Did this group lose out by daring to be squares?

The thrilling conclusion of the training period came as all the trainees stood before the king and conversed with him on a wide range of subjects. Of Daniel and his group the record gives this one-verse thriller: "And in all matters of wisdom and understanding, that the king required of them, he found them *ten times better* [Author's italics] than all the magicians and astrologers that were in all his realm" (v. 20). And an equally thrilling long-time result was that Daniel and his group went very high in governmental circles, became a blessing to the realm, and were a tremendous inspiration and aid to their captive brethren. *It is always better for you, for your influence over others, and for your world that you, too, stick by God-given convictions, regardless of what the other fellows on the team may think or do.*

In the day in which you live, the statistics draw a rather dark picture of the looseness and dissipations of a great throng of young people. Local and national surveys reveal that liquor drinking is equated with smartness and sophistication by millions of people your age; that dishonesty in school relationships runs rampant; that honesty is deemed to be a relevant matter—it is no longer dishonest if the majority do it; that premarital sex experiences are frowned upon only be the "fossils of the past" who have not heard of the "wonderful new morality in sex." In short, now, as in Daniel's time, "King Popularity" has decreed some items in the menu of social relationships that throngs of young people will accept without protest.

But now, as in Daniel's day, there are many young

people your age who are *not* going along with the crowd—a much larger number than you'd think from reading the headlines in newspapers and magazines! Thousands of years of time separate you from Daniel, but the issue is just the same: will you dare to follow the codes of living that will keep your mind and body safe and clean, safeguard your future in vocation and marriage, and offer you the opportunity to bless the very crowd that may unconsciously be honoring you with the lable "square"?

In some ways it is harder for you to carry through on the purpose not to defile yourself than it was for Daniel. Some of the factors that make it harder are these: so many who call themselves Christian are participating in the personality-weakening practices mentioned; newspapers, magazines, radio, and television bring a torrent of wrong action before your eyes, into your ears, and into your mind; so many parents have fallen victim to the easy and popular way out and do not give strong counsel or wise discipline; discordant voices among counselors who help to mold character bring distress and confusion. Though these factors make your struggle for total purity of living a harder one than Daniel's, your victory will be greater, too. Because I believe that the overwhelming majority of young people in America, deep down in their hearts, actually prefer to do right, I point out now the areas or battlefields in which you can win the battle to keep your life clean.

First and most important in this list of battlefields is the mind. The determining effect of *thought* upon the actions of an individual is pointed out so clearly in God's Word and documented so forcefully by the experiences about which you know. Here are just two of the many passages from the Bible, indicating the determining effect of the *mind* (found in God's Word as *heart*):

"Keep thy heart with all diligence; for out of it are the issues of life" (PROVERBS 4:23) .
"But those things which proceed out of the mouth come forth from the heart; and they defile the man. For out of the heart proceed evil thoughts, murders, adulteries, fornications, thefts, false witness, blasphemies: These are the things which defile a man. . ." (MATTHEW 15: 18–2).

That the battle for purity is lost, first, in the individual's heart, if it is lost at all, is documented by the volumes of testimony from the lips of life-stricken people as they have poured out their problems to counselors, court judges, and intimate friends. It is utterly impossible for a person to think below the level of purity over a period of time without giving himself inevitably to defiling practices. *Don't lose this battle!*

The second battlefield for purity in the young person's life is in the area of speech. The twentieth-century youth lives in a flood of profanity of diction, vulgarity of joke and story, and blasphemy of suggestion. The impact of repeated expressions can dull the ear and heart of the average person, so that, almost unconsciously and involuntarily, the expressions he hears constantly can roll off the tongue. But in this important area, as in all other areas, the alert, dedicated, courageous young person can purpose in his heart not to defile himself.

The intelligent young Christian will remember that the glorious wealth of the English language makes it unnecessary to depart from correctness and good taste to express himself clearly and effectively. He will recognize that, in life all about, there is so much good clean wit and humor, that he *never* needs to stoop to the gutter for entertaining material. He will be quick to realize that any blasphemous words or allusions indicate a perverted concept of God and man and indicate a distorted personality—regardless of the temporary popularity of some who seem to thrive on such communications. He will rejoice to find, sooner or later, that even those vulgar in speech admired his purity of speech all along and that, in ridiculing the Christian young person for his "square" pattern of speech, they were not so much condemning him as defending themselves. *If you lose the battle here, you will have lost your opportunity to influence other young people for Christ, despite the fact that your own heart may be basically right.*

The third battlefield in the struggle for personal purity is found in the area of habit life. Here again, the impact of one's day must be remembered; if a young person of our day should pattern his habit life after a large segment of our society he would smoke regularly, despite the irrefutable medical research proving the danger; he would drink alcoholic beverages regularly despite the statistics of the horrifying toll drink takes in physical, mental and spiritual health, in personality deterioration, in marriage breakups and in crime; he would give himself to freedom in sex life, despite the unamended and unrevoked laws of God and the very clear laws of the land regarding sex outside of marriage.

But now, as in Daniel's time, the long-time look will give the young person so much reason for purposing in his heart not to defile himself: he so much wants to be strong of body and healthful in mind; he so much wants nothing to impair his chance of complete success in his vocation; he wants with understandable thrill to have a wonderfully happy marriage—far removed from the divorce courts; he wants to live with self-respect, with respect from his day, and with approval from his God.

Today's Daniel dares to be a "square" in the eyes of the jellyfish crowd; he takes his cues from the good, great Coach of righteousness and not from the loose-playing fellows, a few of whom may be found on the team; he refutes in his living the shallow contention that "everybody's doing it"; *he doesn't have to do it because the crowd is doing it.* He joins the fraternity of the early-day Daniel and finds for himself the glorious rewards of rightliving; and ironically, he finds for the crowd, who will eventually admire his courage and perhaps seek his strength, the sources of strength without which neither he nor they live with victory.

And *you*? Remember that your contract is with Christ and not with the other members of the team. He bought you for His team at the price of His blood. You are a bonus player of the first magnitude. In not letting your great Coach down in your habit life, you will be keeping faith with Him, with yourself, and with the ideals of the game of life!

6

Mighty Mites at Bat

(I Samuel 17:38–50 and Mark 12:41–44)

In every major sport, there have been players of the "peewee" classification—men who were notably undersized but, in many instances, of such magnificent spirit that they have achieved unusual success despite the pessimistic predictions of people who equate importance of potential with mere physical size. Frequently the sports writers have alluded to these small, but powerful players as "mighty mites."

Traditionally, the world has been inclined to undervalue the potential of people and things of small size or unpromising appearance. Even in the area of Christian attitudes this tendency is found. On one occasion when Jesus wanted to feed a multitude of people, his disciples canvassed their resources and found only a lad with five barley loaves and two fishes. One of the disciples, looking at the little lad's lunch through the eyes of man's ability, said in evident despair, "But what are they among so many?" But Jesus looked at the little boy's lunch through the eyes of the infinite power of God and turned it into more than enough food for thousands of people. This lad was one of the earliest of the mighty mites in the history of Christianity.

One of the most fascinating moments in the teaching ministry of Jesus occurred as he and his disciples observed the giving of gifts in the temple treasury. Some came by and dropped in their gold coins ostentatiously. Presently, a simple widow passed by and dropped two mites into the treasury. In the eyes of the world, what she had given was not enough to count. In the eyes of Jesus, she had given the greatest gift: ". . . this poor widow hath cast more in, than all they which have cast into the treasury. For all they did cast in their abundance; but she of her want did cast in all that she had, even all her living" (MARK 12:43–44).

A brilliant mathematician has given us an amazing calculation concerning the potential of the widow's mites. He pointed out that if the widow's mites were valued at one-fourth of a cent and had been invested in A.D. 33 at 4 percent interest, compounded semiannually, the value in the early 1960's would have reached the astronomical figure of: 35 with twenty-nine zeroes following—$3,500,000,000,-000,000,000,000,000,000,000! This same mathematician said that if we should wish to be even more conservative and should value the widow's mites at only one-tenth of a cent, and should have invested it in A.D. 33 at only 2 percent interest, compounded semiannually, the worth of those mites by the early 1960's would have been 38 trillion dollars!

At other times in his ministry Jesus demonstrated the power of the small person or thing, committed to him, multiplied by the power of God:

1) He destroyed forever the effectiveness of the sarcastic question, "Can any good thing come from Nazareth?" Nazareth was a little town, known for its monotony and ordinariness; but touched with the presence of Jesus, it became immortal in word and meaning.

2) Whereas none of the religious leaders of that day would ever have regarded an ignorant, unlearned fisherman as potential for religious leadership, Jesus made of Peter a loving, discerning disciple, the great preacher of Pentecost.

3) Although the religious leaders of the "official"

church of his day thought lofty terms and mysterious figures essential to their teachings, Jesus used the simplest figures and made them mighty forces for teaching: *a little child, a lost coin, lost sheep, a lost boy, lilies of the field, birds of the air, sowing and reaping*; with a simple *basin and towel*, he taught the finest lesson of humility his disciples had ever seen.

4) He taught that acts of service—as small as a cup of water—given in his name, would receive appropriate reward—a lesson gloriously expanded in MATTHEW 25:31–46.

5) In his triumphant death on a crude cross, he turned its meaning from the implication of criminal death to a symbolization of the world's greatest victory.

Down through the history of Christianity, Christ's power has continued to turn little things and people of limited, but committed abilities into mighty mites of spiritual power. That power, added to the prayers of three Christians who were seeking shelter from a sudden rain in a haystack, turned those prayers into the beginning of a great missionary enterprise. That power took William Carey from his cobbler's bench in England to an incomparable missionary career in India. That same power made an uneducated, but committed man—Dwight L. Moody—one of the greatest evangelists of all times. That same power was added to the prayers of a small group of students on a college campus, and a great Christian student movement was the result. And thousands of times this same wonderful power of Christ has made simple Christians the greatest sources of inspiration in their communities and churches.

If you have been feeling that, because of limited abilities, there is little you can do in Christian service, you have failed to remember that this wonderful ability of Christ to turn little things into large blessings is undiminished, and that this power is available to you.

"But what can *I* do that would amount to anything significant?" some reader may be asking. Here are some possibilities:

1) You can *smile*, with the radiance of Christ behind your smile, giving someone cheer and resolution. There have been instances in which individuals were turned back from desperate acts simply because someone cared enough to smile upon them with compassion.

2) You can *speak* a word of encouragement to people who are discouraged, assuring them of your interest and concern. Or you can offer a word of con-

solation to one who has lost a battle, assuring him that the war can still be won.

3) You can *perform the courteous act* which, in turn, will brighten the road of an individual with a heavy load, sending him on his way with a new fragrance in his heart.

4) You can *visit* someone who has experienced sorrow, and share the hope you have in Christ. You may help the grief-stricken person to turn his sorrow into a song of faith.

5) You can *pray* with faith believing; and, with God's power added to that prayer, you may be instrumental in helping other people to lift loads, to solve problems, to achieve victories.

In the realm of sports and in the realm of Christian endeavor, the peewees—the mighty mites—have scored many thrilling victories. Spiritually speaking, if, in the light of your abilities, you feel yourself to be insignificant and without winning potential, why not revise your concepts and convictions in the light of this chapter? Remember: the Giant Goliath was killed—not by the "big boys" on the first team but by a lad named David, who used his simple sling and stones which he had, and this mighty mite won an immortal victory for his team.

7

Woman Player
Saves the Day!

(*The Book of Esther*)

What if the sports section of your newspaper should carry this headline on an article concerning a baseball game: WOMAN PLAYER SAVES THE DAY . . . PULLS GAME OUT OF THE FIRE . . . CALLS WINNING PLAY . . . ? You would probably react with "What's this—am I seeing things?"

In a game of intrigue, presented strikingly in the Book of Esther, a woman player *did* call the winning play and *did* save the day for her Jewish people. Haman, bent upon destroying Esther's kinsman, Mordecai, had tricked King Ahasuerus into an edict that would have made death mandatory for all who did not worship the king. Since Mordecai, Esther, and all devout Jews worshiped only God, Haman evidently rejoiced in having sewed up victory for himself.

Mordecai acquainted Esther with the plot, reminding her that she herself was Jewish; but that, since she had become queen she could appeal to the king to rescind the fatal edict. To go to the king without being bidden was to risk one's life; for if, even to the queen, the king did not extend his scepter, death was the fate. With the elegant touch of a great woman's hand, Esther arranged her approach for a remission of the edict. Chapter 7 of the Book of Esther gives the thrilling climax to this game of intrigue: Esther revealed the reason Haman had obtained the edict; Ahasuerus was furious at Haman and ordered that he be hanged on the very gallows he had gleefully prepared for the hanging of Moredcai.

What can you wonderful young women readers, who come to bat in your own significant ways, glean from the character and experiences of Esther to give you guidance and inspiration in your times of decision making—decisions which determine not only the quality of your lives, but the level of life for society?

First, Esther never forgot who she was. Despite the glamor and glory of being the queen of a powerful monarch, she never failed to remember that she belonged, first of all, to God, and that her prime responsibility was to God and not to the court of which she was queen. She had realized in her own fine heart what Paul voiced to Christians centuries later: ". . . know you not that . . . ye are not your own? For ye are bought with a price . . ." (I CORIN-THIANS 6:19-20). That realization kept her remembering the prior claim of God upon her life and loyalties; this realization, in turn, kept her from losing her way in the fields of limelight and adulation. Esther's contact with God and committal to his control were vital and unbroken.

Similarly, the contemporary young woman Christian will remember that she belongs, first of all, to Christ; that realization will lead her to choose Christ's teachings instead of the crowd's opinions and demands in instances in which the crowd is wrong. She will keep her heart warm with a daily contact with the teachings of Jesus, with continuing communion with him in the fellowship of prayer, and with a perpetual attempt to translate Philippians 1:21 into the reality of living: "For to me to live is Christ. . . ."

Second, Esther never rationalized or temporized her convictions. Instead of replying to Mordecai's request by saying, "You must remember that things have changed. I am now a symbol to people, giving the women of the domain an example by following the king's commands. If I am to influence the domain, I must be identified with it." Instead, without delay or equivocation, she translated her convictions into actions. Had she not held firmly to her deep-seated convictions, the game would have been lost for both herself and her people throughout a vast domain of 127 provinces. *So much depended on her maintaining her convictions in that faraway century!*

In your day, the impact of standing by your convictions firmly and radiantly is even stronger; for, indeed, in our society, woman's position of esteem makes possible her determining more fully than ever before in history the level of society's character and morality.

In my many years of observing "the way of a maid with a man," I have been amazed and thrilled by the complete transformation of ideals and behavior in the lives of young men who have come to admire, love, and trust wonderful Christian girls. Occasionally one may find that a marriage in which the man is the strong Christian becomes a strong Christian marriage, but in a multitude of instances it is a glorious Christian wife who creates and strengthens a vital, Christian family life. In daily living, in the happy experience of dating, in the long-time relationship of marriage, *you* can be the woman player who changes the course of the game from defeat to victory—for yourself and for others!

Third, Esther demonstrated the courage of a great woman in risking her very life upon the mood and whim of a king, who might well not extend his scepter! Our English word "courage" comes from the Latin word *cors,* which actually means "heart." Therefore, courage is that kind of heart which is strong enough to dare to do right even at great risk—to dare to undertake a challenge or responsibility that may cost one's life or popularity or fortune.

Courage and cowardice stand in stark contrast, and every Christian chooses between the two in moments of decision involving principle. The courageous ones have not always won their battles immediately; some have died on the stake, some by the mouths of wild beasts in the coliseums, on crosses of crucifixion, in dungeons and on wheels of torture; yet, history has vindicated them and condemned their persecutors. Risking so much in being a martyr isn't pleasant in any age, but it is imperative to committed Christian living in every age.

The circumstances under which you may be called upon to demonstrate great courage may not be under the spotlights of publicity; it may even occur when you and one other person are alone and hidden from the world; but the need for courage is the same, the heroism of courage is the same, and the blessings to self and to others are the same.

There have been many other women in history who have joined Esther in saving the day, staging the winning play of the game. Moses' mother risked the ire and doom of Pharaoh, when she refused to destroy her young son at the order of the monarch. Deborah dared to follow the will of God in political and spiritual leadership as a judge and in military leadership with Barak, despite the fact that women hardly ever filled those roles. Joan of Arc, Nurse Edith Cavell in World War I, Carrie Nation in her unremitting fight against the curse of liquor, Jane Addams in her compassion-filled leadership in sociological reform, and many other women whose hallmark has been high courage are in the galaxy of women of the Esther tradition. Their influence is everlasting, and their names are immortal.

Closer to you young women who read these lines are many high-school and college girls who, though chosen for queenships and similar honors, comport themselves with radiance in uncompromising behavior. They create new images of *queen*; they inspire and lead crowds instead of concurring with the crowd and losing their identities as ideals-givers and symbols. There are those, some of whom you know, who have transformed sororities, dormitories, and even campuses because of their Christ-contact, convictions, and courage.

Mordecai, Esther's kinsman, said to her in urging her to go to the king, even at the risk of her life: ". . . and who knoweth whether thou art come to the kingdom for such a time as this?" (ESTHER 4:14b). Who knows, wonderful young woman reader, but that *you* are the girl to make the winning play, to save the game for yourself and others of your crowd, school, or day? It could be that if you don't maintain contact with, and committal to, Christ, if you don't hold firmly and radiantly to your conviction, if you don't demonstrate the courage of Esther, the whole tone of the social stratum of which you are a part may lose the game and become a society of weakness and mediocrity. If you want to be genuinely and abidingly admired, remembered and honored by posterity, you will find Esther's pattern of courage the sure way.

Only *you* can make the choice between becoming a cheap, but temporary queen or becoming a courageous, danger-facing queen whose name and influence will be immortal. Wouldn't you like the headlines of God's records to read: "WOMAN PLAYER SAVES THE DAY . . . PULLS THE GAME OUT OF THE FIRE . . . STAGES THE WINNING PLAY?" Though you'll probably never get to stage that feat on a baseball diamond, you *can* perform it on the diamond of life, on which women can play as heroically as men!

8

Don't Strike Out Here!

(Matthew 28:18–20 and Psalms 107:2)

Dr. Elton Trueblood, distinguished philosopher and author, has written a number of excellent books. In one of them, which bears the pungent title *Your Other Vocation,* he points out that, during the early days of Christianity, regardless of the vocation in which a Christian earned his living, his *other vocation* was the sharing of his knowledge of Jesus with other people.

As the centuries have passed, however, there has been a tendency to commit Christian witnessing to the ministers, missionaries, and paid church workers. It is clear, though, that Jesus expects that the *other vocation* of every Christian shall be the sharing of his knowledge of Christ with others.

Many of you are now enrolled at various levels of educational institutions. Right now your official

69

vocation (as was mine just a few years ago) is *student*. You are in the process of preparing yourself, doubtless, for a vocation into which you will go later to earn your livelihood; but, even now, if you are a Christian, your *other vocation* is the telling of other people about Jesus.

How shall the individual proceed to practice this *other vocation?* Although every Christian will want to fulfill this hope of Jesus according to individual abilities and opportunities, there are two ways through which *all* Christians can practice that important *other vocation*.

All Christians can witness through example, through striving to be Christlike in our daily living: in classrooms, in dormitories, in our social lives, on the athletic fields, in places in which we work—in short, *everywhere*! Or, in the words of a well-known chorus sung by young people in youth gatherings the Christian will say, "Only to be what *He* wants me to be, every moment of every day."

I know of a student who attended a high school with an enrollment of over 2,000 students, who lived such a winsome Christian life that he molded the thinking and conduct of the entire student body of that large high school.

In a stenographers' pool of a large concern there

was a young woman who lived the teachings and spirit of Jesus in such a radiant and convincing way, that the fifty girls in that particular group came to her for counsel and inspiration.

Many men in military service have so lived the teachings and spirit of Christ that the spirit and attitudes in entire barracks have been changed—not because of what the men said, but because they dared to *live* their Christianity daily.

Many years ago, a group of college students attending a retreat wanted to formulate an expression of purpose to remind themselves of the importance of daily Christian living as a means of witnessing. The expression of purpose agreed upon and tucked into the hearts of hundreds of students as they went back to their far-flung campuses was this: "Relying upon divine aid, I purpose so to live Christ on my campus, that if I were the only Christian on it, others might come to know Christ through me." It would be highly profitable for every reader to apply that statement of purpose to his own present daily associations at school, or at work, or in leisure-time activities.

The power of example in daily Christian living is almost inexpressibly significant; for, indeed, nothing the lips of the Christian may say concerning Christ will be effective if the Christian's life does not demonstrate the spirit and teachings of Jesus.

Indispensable as example is in the practicing of that other vocation, example alone is not enough. Although the example which Christ's life gave was perfect, evidently he did not regard example alone as sufficient. You will recall that he witnessed constantly with his lips, telling individuals and groups of the wonderful heavenly Father. Therefore, the Christian who says, "I witness with my life and do not need to be talking to other people about Christ," is actually presumptuous: he is saying, in effect, that his example is accomplishing what the example of Jesus did not accomplish without witnessing with verbal power!

Verbal witnessing to other people is an imperative phase of practicing one's *other vocation*. At the outset of his ministry, Jesus gave an unmistakable and inescapable challenge to personal witnessing. "Ye are the light of the world," are the words Jesus used to express the hope that you and I will live lives of such total commitment and speak words of such winsome persuasiveness that our buddies, pals, and all other associates will come to know Jesus.

In his final hours of fellowship with his disciples, Jesus gave what has come to be called "The Great Commission," in which he specified that his followers should share the gospel with every creature. *Preach* and *teach* are emphasized in these parting words; therefore, witnessing by word as well as by example is expected of us.

I know a public health nurse who is practicing her *other vocation* wonderfully. She is assigned to an underprivileged area of a large city, and in this area she ministers to the needs of many people. She never passes up an opportunity to share her knowledge of Jesus with individuals to whom she ministers. As a result, she has acquainted many of the people with Christ, some of whom had actually not known of his love and care. She has taken seriously her *other vocation*.

Too, I have heard of a traveling salesman who makes radiant contacts with hotel and motel personnel in his days of lodging and dining, sharing through his wonderful spirit and verbal testimony a forceful Christian witness. I have heard, also, of many students who build friendships with non-Christian students, using this rapport to tell these fellow-students the good news of Christ. In other words, at least some followers of Christ in the twentieth century have been emulating their forebears of the first century in making Christian witnessing their *other vocation*!

A THRILLING POSSIBILITY

If *one* Christian should decide to win one other person to Christ each year from now forward, and should challenge each one he wins to win one other each year, asking all of them to challenge all the people they win to follow that pattern of witnessing, do you know how many new Christians there would be at the end of twenty-five years?

The sequence would move slowly at first: you and the one you had won during the first year, then 4—8—16—32—64—128. Beginning with just *you* this year, in twenty-five years over 33,000,000 people would have been won to Christ!

And what if winning other people to faith in Christ should become "the other vocation" of one hundred other readers of this book—of a thousand Christians? The answer is simply this: the world would be won to Christ in a matter of decades. You are not responsible for what other Christians may do about this important matter, but *you* can let witnessing become *your other vocation.*

A HAUNTING REMINDER

A writer of many years ago used his excellent powers of imagination to picture the return of Jesus to Heaven and the concern of the chief angels that his sacrifice on earth not be lost in any way. One of the angels is reported to have asked, "Master, what plan did you leave on the earth whereby the people shall come to know of the salvation which you made possible?" The writer imagined that Jesus, smiling confidently, replied, "I left Peter, John, and the other faithful disciples; they will tell others about me, and those others will tell others. . . ." One of the chief angels, not quite satisfied that the gospel would get through, persisted: "But, Master, what if those followers fail you?" The writer pictures Jesus' smile of confidence in replying: "If my followers fail me, I have absolutely no other plan."

And so it is, reading friend, if you and I should fail to practice our *other vocation,* we shall have failed in fulfilling the fervent and urgent hope of Jesus concerning the relaying of his message. If you have never begun to practice that wonderful *other vocation,* why not come to bat in this regard *now?* In this witnessing inning you will experience joy and thrill which you haven't experienced before.

Don't strike out here!

(Additional readings: ACTS 5:42 and DANIEL 12:3)

9

The Original Beatle at Bat
—And Out!

(Judges 14–16)

In the furor of excitement concerning the British
musical group, widely heralded as The Beatles, I
found it difficult to refrain from telling my many
young friends of Beatle-mania that the British
Beatles were really "old hat"; for long, long ago the
original Beatle strode across the stage and created an
almost incredible wave of admiration, wonder, and
fear. His name was Samson. "Beatle?" you ask in
perplexity. "I think so," I reply facetiously, "because, after all, he did have long hair; he 'fiddled
around' considerably; he wowed the girls; and he
made all the boys envious!"

In a more serious vein, Samson did come to bat at
a moment in the history of his people in which he
could have performed a memorable career of leadership; for, without kings at that time, the Children of

Israel depended upon strong men called "Judges" to lead them. Samson had deeply religious parents, who sought to steer him into wiser dating relationships. He was a man of unusual physical prowess and evident leadership capacity. His people had need of a strong and trustworthy leader in their continuing struggle against the Philistines. Yet, Samson, faced with a magnificent opportunity of leadership and victory, struck out when he came to bat, because he insisted on dating the wrong sort of girls and upon marrying the wrong type of woman. The sad dissipation of his wonderful strength and the tragic climax of what might have been a wonderful life are set forth in the Bible passage suggested at the beginning of this chapter.

Samson's type, found in every century, is found among us today. There are many young people with splendid personalities and great potential, of correct vocational choice and superlatively fine training, who strike out because they date and marry persons with whom they cannot build marriages or careers of stability and success. Feeling that you young men and women who read these lines do *not* want to strike out in this vastly important inning of your lives, I am offering three suggestions I've seen work over the years, and which can be helpful in your ideals for dating and marriage.

First, seek God's guidance carefully, patiently. Since God himself established marriage in making Adam and Eve for each other, it must matter to him *whom* you marry. In view of the catastrophic number of marriages which break up each year in our nation, it is evident that a vast number of young people either have not asked God for guidance in this all-important area of their lives, or that they have not waited to receive the guidance.

It is as important that you seek God's guidance concerning whom to marry as it is to seek his guidance concerning what vocation to follow. "But," you say, "choosing a vocation is a choice for a lifelong investment." But, is it not true, young friend, that God means that marriage shall be a "till death doth us part" investment? Although some today seem to follow the marriage practice of "if it doesn't work, off with the old and on with the new," that is not God's concept of marriage for you. Since He *does* wish the marriage decision to be a lifelong one, and since he knows so much better than you or I what the demands of the future will be, it matters all the more that his guidance be sought in this vastly important decision.

If you are now only a teen-ager, you can pray that, in His time and in His way, God will so direct and lead you that you will meet the person whom you ought to marry. When your heart begins to feel sensations toward a member of the opposite sex, which run beyond the sensations of friendship, ask God again to help you to *know* in unmistakable ways whether this is just *a* love or *the* love—the one that will not only last a lifetime, but will become more wonderful with the passing years. If you will ask honestly, not just to get a confirmation of your desires, but to know God's will with commitment to follow it, the guidance will come. And, before declaring love or planning marriage, you will be wise to be equally sure that God's will has been found.

Second, take your time in deciding this important matter and in entering this tremendously important relationship. Given good health, you and your lifemate can expect forty or fifty years of joyous marriage. So, there is plenty of time to enjoy marriage— so much time, in fact, that if a wrong choice is made, it's a ghastly long time to endure! Take your time in these two significant aspects:

Take your time in seeking, finding, and deciding the matter of whom to marry. The old adage, "marry in haste, repent at leisure," is too

tragically true to be humorous. Putting your
love to the time test will prove whether it is
mere infatuation or genuine love; for infatuation never lasts, intense though it be for a time.
The time test will make it possible, too, for the
two of you to discuss ideals and practical considerations at an intelligent length; to associate
with each other under a sufficient variety of circumstances of tension, disappointment, and
readjustment, so that each of you will *know*
how the other reacts to such circumstances; to
know through times of prayer and Bible-study
together how deep or shallow the spiritual
capacities are.

Take your time, too, in making sure that you
have developed the maturities and achieved the
preparations necessary for resourcefulness in
marriage.

You are aware, doubtless, of the tremendous
amount of care the air lines of our nation exer-
cise in selecting and training the personnel who
will fly their planes. In selection, much consid-
eration is given to stability of character, trust-
worthiness, intelligence, and capacity for training and maturing. In the arduous training pe-

riod, every conceivable preparation is required, so that the pilots are prepared not only for all of the normal responsibilities of successful flight, but for eventualities and emergencies as well. Priceless lives and valuable cargoes are in the hands of these men!

Similarly, marriage is a flight into the "wild blue yonder" of an unknown future, and its successful conduct will depend upon the quality of its copilots. In the normal pattern of marriage, there will be eventual "passengers" in the coming of precious children. Instability, immaturity, untrustworthiness on the part of either or both of the pilots can make this marriage flight unhappy or even tragic for both pilots and passengers.

Therefore, whatever time is required for your preparation as a copilot in a meant-to-be-joyous marriage journey is not too much or too long. That fine wisdom down in your heart tells you that you do not want to be responsible for a crash which will mar your life and maim the lives of others for whom you are responsible.

So, young friend, your marriage will be either a successful flight with joy to you, to your copilot, and to the God-given passengers; or it will be an unhappy flight with possible tragedy for everyone involved: it depends upon how much personality, maturity, and resourcefulness you bring to your marriage. Therefore, you will be wise to take all the time needed to get adequate education, to develop maturity of mind and heart, to know intelligently what a marriage of successful nature demands, and to be willing to give yourself completely to making of marriage a thrilling venture of lifelong dimensions.

Third, when you think that your feeling for another person is love, listen to your head as well as to your heart. Although head and heart make different approaches, each is indispensable to the other; and a marriage decision made by the one without concurrence of the other is likely not to be well balanced and, therefore, inadequate.

While your heart overflows with the joyous romantic feeling that causes you to feel that "you'd just die" if you couldn't spend all the rest of your life with your beloved, listen to some questions the head is asking:

"Are we old enough to be mature enough to understand the demands of marriage?"

"Do we have adequate preparation for marriage through education, insight, and responsibility?"

"Do I believe that he is in the best vocation in the world for him? . . . and can I be enthusiastic for his work through the years."

"Do I believe that she will be a wife of understanding, companionship, and helpfulness?"

"Will she be a wonderful mother? . . . Will he be an admirable dad."

"Have we known each other long enough under a sufficient variety of tensions, pressures, and disappointments to know that we like each other even when things go wrong? . . . When she is wrong? . . . When he is wrong."

"Do we *know* that both of us are genuine Christians, dedicated to making our individual lives, our marriage, our family, his career assets to the cause of Christ? Do we enjoy devotional times together? Do we inspire each other to want to be the maximum in Christian living?"

"Are there character weaknesses or habits in either life which give concern to the other, as we contemplate the heavy exactions of character strength which marriage will make?"

"Have we permitted God to reveal his will to us in ways which will make doubt about the rightness of our marriage forever impossible, and that, therefore, we feel that life for both of us would miss God's planned fulfillment if we should miss marrying each other?"

Sufficient thinking, praying, waiting, planning, preparing, and knowing prior to marriage will insure that you will not strike out in this great inning called marriage. The tragedy of Samson's "out" will not be repeated in the life of any young person who seeks and follows God's will!

10

Three Strikes, But Not Out!

(II Corinthians 11:23–28, Philippians 4:13)

To the man at bat in a baseball game, the words, "Strike three: you're out!", are gloom-giving words, indeed. For the man at bat, those words from the umpire mean that, for the present, the player has no additional opportunity to score for his team. He hopes to come to bat again in the course of the game; but, for the present, he's *out,* and that's final.

Although all of that is true in the game of baseball, there is a remarkable difference in the broader game of life when circumstances call three strikes against an individual. In the game of life the player is definitely not *out* unless he stops trying. There are so many people of earlier days and of our own day against whom handicaps, failures or mistakes, and severe losses were called "strike three" but whose glorious records show that they were, most surely, not *out*. Let's listen to some of their true-to-life stories.

STRIKE ONE: PHYSICAL HANDICAPS

Physical handicaps of tremendous dimensions have come to many people; yet some of these stricken ones have achieved such inspiring triumphs over their handicaps, that spectators have been lifted to high degrees of enthusiasm and admiration.

All of us remember Helen Keller with highest regard. The series of illnesses in her infancy that brought her deafness, blindness, and the inability to talk were three strikes, if ever there could be! Yet, thanks to a magnificent teacher, patience, continuing efforts, and a will to break through the barriers which separated her from her world, Helen Keller learned to talk, to read, to write, to travel, and to proceed upon a journey toward world fame.

A courageous young man battled crippling polio and achieved a limited ability to walk, only to face great impairment of his eyesight. Undaunted, he went along to college; and, though every physical step and every intellectual step forward necessitated all of his strength, he never once thought of turning back. As he approached his senior year, a medical diagnosis revealed that he had tuberculosis, and he had to go to a distant hospital to recover. These three strikes, plus the loss of his beloved mother, did not send him out of the game, however; and to the delight and admiration of all his fans, he returned to college and received his degree.

Ben Hogan in golf, Brian Sternberg in pole vaulting, and Ron Manka in basketball—all outstanding in their sports and all three tragically handicapped by accidents—have inspired America with their "three strikes, but not out" spirit and have led many with lesser handicaps to try again.

There are many others whose stories could be told with profit to all of us. Some are in iron lungs, but graduating from college. Some are blind, bedridden, detached from their world, but achieving victories and dispensing cheer. Three strikes have been called against them, but they are definitely not *out!*

STRIKE TWO: FAILURES AND MISTAKES

A second group of people against whom three strikes have been called, but who have not been *out* are those who have experienced successive failures or who have made serious mistakes in their journey forward. Kentucky and Illinois gave to our nation a young man who, despite a succession of seven failures, was never *out*. He kept going forward, despite his failures, to become President Abraham Lincoln. In the field of research, in the field of writing, and in many other areas of endeavor, courageous men and women have kept striving despite failures, frustrations, rejection slips, and disappointed hopes. Because of their "three strikes, but not out" courage, the whole world has been blessed.

Have you felt discouraged and tempted to quit some worthwhile undertaking because you have suffered some failures? If that is your state of mind now, or if that should come to be your feeling in the future, just remember that three strikes of failure do not *have* to put you out of the game, and that they will not do so unless you permit them to.

Mistakes, too, have hounded many people with the impulse to quit the game; and, quite naturally, some have thrown down their bats and left the game in defeat, not waiting for later chances to come to bat. Others, however, have admitted their mistakes, have learned much from them, and have continued in the game to phenomenal successes.

Remember Peter, one of Christ's most devoted disciples, and his tremendous mistake on the night of Christ's trial? Although he had vowed that he would stick by his Lord, even if death were the cost, he denied him three times outside the chamber of trial. Realizing his mistake, Peter repented, confessed, and tried again to demonstrate his love and loyalty. Christ, always tender-hearted toward people who make mistakes and who want to do better, not only forgave Peter, but permitted him to become the great preacher of Pentecost. What if Peter, having made that dreadful mistake three times in one night, had thrown down his bat and left the game? Christianity would have lost one of its most heroic leaders!

Other people with whom Jesus had contact had made serious mistakes, but were evidently still looking for better ways of living: The woman at the well of Sychar, who had disobeyed the laws of God and man in multiple marriages and evil living; Zaccheus, who had made countless dishonest business transactions; the woman caught in the act of adultery and threatened with stoning by the men who dragged her into the presence of Jesus; Paul, who, prior to his conversion, had been Christianity's most venomous antagonist. All of these had made serious mistakes, but Christ forgave them and helped them to live lives of usefulness.

Some of America's most inspiring and useful citizens of today are people who, in earlier years made serious mistakes but did not permit three strikes to be their finale. There are wonderful preachers now in pulpits who were disciplined in high school or suspended from college years ago. There are public-school teachers of great usefulness who themselves were problem students years ago. There are men and women in many areas of usefulness in our day who formerly made mistakes serious enough to draw court censures, but they have not permitted these mistakes of the past to keep them from reentering the game of life with a disciplined spirit and a will to win.

STRIKE THREE: TERRIFIC LOSSES

A final group of wonderful people who have had three strikes called against them, but who are definitely not *out*, are those who have suffered terrific losses, yet have kept going forward to victory.

A wonderful college teacher lost three members of his family in death in the space of eighteen months. The deaths were particularly heartbreaking losses, because two of them were the deaths of his much-loved sons. Despite fears of friends that his own strength would break, he kept in the game, and he moved straight forward to thrilling victories. He began work on a doctorate in his field, did the work in minimum time and with highest academic quality, received a succession of accolades, and returned to his college teaching position with a spirit of radiance which challenges all of his associates not to let three strikes mean *out!*

Others, who have suffered terrible losses in other ways, have not permitted these losses—often total and terrific—to cause them to throw down their bats of purpose and leave the game: loss of health which necessitated loss of position or career, loss of material wealth to the point of totality, loss of husband or wife or family through tragic accident, or loss of achievement when it was very close to fulfillment. When the umpire of circumstances shouted, "Three strikes, you're out!", they understood that he meant *for now*, not *forever!*

AND YOU?

So, team member, if you have been discouraged by the strikes that are mounting up against you, take courage from the wonderful people about whom we have just heard. They had access to no more power than that available to you as a Christian; for you, too, have access to the power, wisdom, presence, and love of God. Your resolution to keep on trying *plus* the dimensions which God will add to your efforts will assure that, though circumstances may call three strikes on you, they do not have to put you out of the game.

11

Benched and Blushing!

(Psalms 15, and Proverbs 16:32)

In recent years, gifted players have had to be withdrawn from play in several major sports—some of them for the remainder of the season—because of loss of temper control, which loss brought on unsportsmanlike conduct. "Benched and blushing" is an accurate description of the plight of those players.

One of the greatest challenges, in sports and in life, is that of keeping normal desires and drives within the bounds of wholesome motivation. So often, a perfectly right desire, if undisciplined, can grow to dimensions which make it a destructive monster instead of a wholesome motivation—*ambition*, for instance.

Ambition is one of the most normal drives of life: the desire to do well, to succeed, to excel. As long as desire simply impels the individual to strive with all of his powers, it is a wholesome motivation; it will evoke the highest energies, the finest courage, and the fullest use and development of one's abilities. Yet, if desire gets out of bounds to the degree that *winning at any cost* is sought, what began as a normal motivation may well grow into *greed, jealousy, envy, hatred,* and even into the lowest of desires— *the desire to harm other players* in the game of life, whose achievements have won victory and acclaim.

Greed has led once wholesome people into a loss of honorable value systems and into actions that appall and revolt former admirers. The greed may be for money, for social acclaim, for political influence, for friends, for fame, or for any one of a great variety of things.

A man once told me of a college buddy whom he had admired during college days, who, upon entering a business career, developed such greed that nothing short of the destruction of his competitors seemed to satisfy him. At the twenty-fifth anniversary reunion of their college class, this immensely wealthy classmate appeared with the evident intention to outdress, outbrag, and outflash all of his contemporaries. According to the alumnus who shared the story with me, the consuming greed of this fellow-alumnus so showed in his eyes, face, and manner that he became revolting to all his former classmates.

Jealousy has led erstwhile good people to heart-blackening emotions and to subsequent actions which broke hearts and lives. In one woman's life, jealousy ruined the professional career of her husband, drove their children to maladjustment, and eventually sent the woman herself to a mental institution. The jealousy in a workman's life drove him to murder his children, and to commit suicide in a tragic attempt to strike back at imagined actions in his wife's life. Jealousy in the lives of young people has often impelled them to behave unworthily—at times, to life-shattering actions.

Envy can drive basically good players into words and actions that make them poor sports, and to actions which disappoint their fans greatly. An interesting Greek myth tells of an envy-ridden runner whose envy toward the winner of a marathon led to an unworthy act and to his own destruction. A large stone marker had been erected in a public place in honor of the winner's triumph. Envy so possessed the loser that he undertook a sorry mission: he crept out one night to try to pull the marker from its base to crush it to pieces. In the attempt, however, he tripped, and the huge stone marker fell upon him and crushed him to death. At dawn the whole city saw the tragedy of envy's efforts.

Hate impairs the physical, mental, and spiritual health of the individual who entertains it; and, sadder still, hate can lead to the desire and the effort to hurt other people. Characters have been impugned, reputations have been shattered, marriages have been wrecked, businesses have been destroyed, murder and suicide have been done, and even catastrophic wars that were sparked by hate in individuals' hearts. Hate in an individual's heart will cost *him* so much. Hate in one person's heart can cost other people even more. Hate is, indeed, the most destructive emotion which enters the human heart, and no player in the game of life will ever be a winner with hate in his heart.

Any one of the foregoing emotions can bench the best of players and leave the benched player blushing through the years!

HOLD THAT LINE!

Another drive which, when undisciplined, can become a destructive master instead of an enriching asset is *temper*. Temper is comparable to steam and electricity: When controlled and directed, those two powers become wonderful servants of a vast array of human needs; uncontrolled, they become instantly and tragically destructive. Temper, properly controlled and disciplined, adds zest, verve, dynamic, and leadership capacity to an individual's personality. When undisciplined and uncontrolled, however, temper can destroy an individual's attractiveness and usefulness.

Uncontrolled temper can rob one of friendships, can consign one to a lesser level of vocational usefulness than his abilities merit, can wreck a meant-to-be wonderful marriage, can make a murderer out of a person who, in a state of temper control, would never have done violence to anyone. There are many with broken hearts, with shattered lives, with problems of mental health, and many in prisons who would never have been tragedy smitten, unwell, or imprisoned, had they disciplined temper.

Isn't it sad that many potential All-Americans in sports and in daily living have been benched, shamed, and defeated by an uncontrolled personality trait which, had it been disciplined and controlled, could have made immortal winners of them? And wouldn't it be doubly sad if some of you, warned by the examples of players who did not "hold that line," should fail to bring temper under discipline and control and should, therefore, be benched and shamed in the game of life which you much want to win?

THE GREATEST TEST

Many of us remember that, in a recent year, a man holding a high government position in another nation, his future resplendent with promise, fell in disgrace when it was discovered that he had carried on an illicit sex affair and had lied to the legislative body concerning the affair. To follow the language of our chapter title, he was called from the game at the height of successful performance—benched and blushing, because a basically good drive had been permitted to express itself illicitly.

There is, perhaps, no God-given drive more tragically diverted from its God-intended use in contemporary life than sex. If disciplined through wholesome thought and will power, and if saved for gratification in a love-permeated marriage, this drive brings incomparable joy and blessing. However, if this drive is permitted to possess an individual's thoughts and emotions in an undisciplined manner, it can be his undoing—make an animal of him, wreck his life, bring shame to a varsity-potential player, and hurt others, at the height of what could have been an inspiring career.

The same Creator who gave us the sex drive for completely wholesome purposes, gave to us, also, three other dimensions or resources with which to discipline that drive: *reason, conscience,* and *will power.* Reason speaks to tell us that tampering with sex is dangerous. Conscience speaks in still, but firm tones to tell us that a misuse of sex is wrong. Will power speaks up to remind us that it is God's gift to us to help us to keep the sex drive under control until the joyous relationship of marriage makes possible its intended use.

If reason, conscience, and will power are heeded, one of life's finest victories is achieved. If these three God-given resources are not called into play in dealing with one's sex drive, any first-stringer on the team of this game of life can be called from glamur to gloom, from success to shame—or, to say it again, from the battle to the bench.

In the spirit of ECCLESIASTES 12:1; "Let us hear the conclusion of the whole matter." And conclude the whole matter by repeating the key verse (PROVERBS 16:23) with which this chapter began: *"He that is slow to anger is better than the mighty; and he that ruleth his spirit than he that taketh a city."*

12

The Topflight Player

(John 6:5-13)

Let's think for a while about that much talked-about subject, *success*. Everybody who is normal wants to live a successful life. An evidence of our personal interest in success is that, when someone has accomplished unusually well, all of us want to know the formula which helped that individual achieve success.

All of us who have participated in athletics realize that the athlete who has achieved success is, normally, a person with good basic athletic ability, who has submitted to the direction of a coach of seasoned ability and experience. Likewise, if the young Christian wishes to achieve maximum success in his total life pattern, it will be necessary for him to follow the pattern of conditioning and development presented so clearly in the teachings of Jesus, the Master Coach of successful living. Is there such a pattern in the teachings of Jesus? There is, and it is found in the Bible passage listed at the beginning of this chapter.

You will recall that in that passage a small boy placed in the hands of Jesus all he had: a lunch of five barley loaves and two little fish. The result of that commitment, plus the power which Jesus added to it, was that five thousand people were fed so generously that baskets of food were left over. If you please, the little boy gave himself to a need of Christianity at the moment, and Jesus multiplied his life to a usefulness far beyond the hopes and imaginations of the boy. The boy himself could not have multiplied his life to those dimensions, nor could the crowd have done it, but Jesus could and did!

Therefore, we may deduce from this episode the formula for becoming a topflight player in this game of life. *If we want to experience maximum success, as God views success, we must be willing to turn all of our God-given abilities over to the control of Christ, just as the lad did with his lunch long ago.*

Some years ago, I heard or read this graphic illustration: a five-pound bar of steel could be turned into articles that varied in total sales value from $10.50 to $2,500, depending upon how the bar of steel was used.

If the five-pound bar of steel were used in making

horseshoes, it would produce $10.50 worth of horseshoes. If it were used in making high quality steel pins, which go into machinery, it would produce $350 worth of pins. But if the same bar of steel were used in making the highest quality watch springs, it would produce a minimum of $2,500 worth of such springs. To think that the ultimate value of that bar of steel could vary from $10.50 to $2,500; depending upon whose hands control it—blacksmith or watchmaker!

The same truths can be pointed out in other material areas. A piece of wood, for instance, may be only a board to you and me; yet, in the hands of a skillful wood-carver, it can become a wood carving of lasting beauty. A stone, trodden underfoot by most of us, committed to the hands of the gifted sculptor can become a work of art. Clay, simply "underfooting" to most of us—and often a nuisance —placed in the hands of the experienced potter can become pottery of beauty and usefulness.

From the background of those illustrations, let's look at three possible commitments from which the individual must choose for the control of his life; the choice of the force to which one's life is committed for control will determine whether he will become a *topflight* player or just a player on the team of everyday living.

First, an individual can surrender his life to his own selfish desires and become exactly what he wants to become, regardless of the wishes of the Master Coach for his life. This first possibility is comparable to using the steel bar to produce horseshoes, worth, as you recall, only $10.50: a cheap use of life material which, if put to higher uses, could produce much more of value. It is ironical that the individual who surrenders his life to his own selfish whims fails miserably to achieve lasting gratification. Like the Prodigal Son in Christ's parable, eventually he "comes to himself" in realizing that self-indulgence is shortsighted and leads only to frustration and disappointment, despite the bright promises and deep thrills this way of life seemed to indicate.

Second, the same individual may choose to surrender his life to the ideals and ways of his world, succumbing to the pressures of the crowd, the pressures to conform even to wrong concepts and practices of the crowd. Doubtless, this is the greatest pressure young people face today. The wise individual will recognize, however, that surrendering his life to the demands of the crowd will achieve only a temporary popularity. Although this popularity may be gratifying at the time, he will recognize that, in the long run, the crowd which cheers today is likely to forget tomorrow—leaving yesterday's heroes frustrated and empty.

At this point, a reminder from our "Squeeze Play" chapter may be useful. The crowd, from which the topflight player has dared to be different, may reward him at the time with isolation, ridicule, or rejection; yet some, perhaps many, will secretly admire the courageous young person for daring to go it alone in preference to compromising his Christian convictions. Some of these secret admirers may well become ardent advocates of courageous living, too. In so becoming, they will have joined in refusing to surrender their lives to the control of the ideals of the world. They, too, will have saved their lives for a commitment to a still higher and better control.

Third, the possibility for the surrender of one's life is clear: the placing of one's life in the wonderful hands of Jesus, permitting Him to control life to such an extent that its significance is multiplied to dimensions comparable to the little lad's lunch and to the use of that bar of steel for producing high-quality watch springs. This commitment of life to the control of the Master Coach brings usefulness and joy beyond the fondest hopes and dreams of the individual.

Some people in our world of today have made this third and highest commitment. Billy Graham, an unknown North Carolina boy at conversion, is now the best-known evangelist of our day. Why? Simply put, he realized the importance of turning his life over to the wonderful control of Christ; and, because he made a complete committal, God has multiplied his life to a usefulness beyond anything Billy Graham or a crowd-controlling commitment could have accomplished. Florence Nightingale, the founder of modern nursing, said on one occasion: "It amazes me to see what God can do with the life of a simple woman, if that life is dedicated to him." Dr. George Washington Carver, distinguished scientist, interpreted his phenomenal success in chemurgical research as the result of being a committed medium through which God could work.

In conclusion, I want to share with you the experience of a young man who achieved maximum success, though his life-span lasted only eighteen years. He was a senior in a Mississippi high school and was editor of the school paper. One day, as he was returning from a nearby community with proofs of that week's student newspaper, the little foreign car his parents had provided for his busy senior year turned over. Because he was alone, no one knows exactly what occurred, but the tragic result of the accident was Bob's instant death.

From the pocket of his sports shirt two items were

taken: a little New Testament, which gave evidence of having been read faithfully, and a note card. On one side of the card Bob had written his chores for that day. On the other side of the card he had written these words: "You must be careful of the life you lead: you are the only Bible some people will read."

Upon hearing of Bob's death, the entire student body of more than a thousand was plunged into grief. Students told their friends, parents and newspaper reporters that when they thought of Bob Cook, they thought of Christianity automatically. They felt him to be the best Christian in their school.

On the day of Bob's funeral, the city's largest daily newspaper carried as its first editorial a tribute to Bob Cook. The editor repeated the words found on the note card: "You must be careful of the life you lead: you are the only Bible some people will read." Another editor, commenting upon the effectiveness of Bob's life, observed wisely: "If there were more Christians *like* Bob Cook in our world today, there would be more Christians *in* our world."

The secret of the life of Bob Cook is the secret which has made topflight players of so many young people in the history of Christianity: he made a total commitment of his life to the control of Christ, the Master Coach—the secret of how the long-ago lad became a blessing to thousands of people.

How much of *your* life remains to be committed to the great Master Coach of the game of life? The quantity of your life controlled by Christ will determine your place on the roster of players on *His* team. As of now, are you just one of the players, or are you one of the *topflight* players? *You can be a topflight player if, with all your heart, you want to be!*

13

The Topflight Coach

(Matthew 16:13–17)

Sometimes in the realm of sports, new candidates for the team regard the coach with some degree of wholesome fear. In all probability, these candidates have heard that this coach has unusually high expectations of the men who play under his direction and a very strict regimen for their training. But, as they come to know this coach and to respect him for his strength of character and his skill in coaching, they come to admire him greatly; and, interestingly enough, they then regard his high ideals and strict regimen for the players as fully justified.

More likely than not, there are some excellent prospects for the sport this coach directs who never come to know him for his goodness and wisdom, because they permit unjustified fears and shallow hearsay to keep them from going out for the team. Their loss is great, for the coach is far more wonderful than they realize.

Similarly, in the area of Christian living there are many young people of high potential who are apparently reluctant to submit themselves fully to the high ideals and wise regimen of the Master Coach, because they, too, have permitted unjustified fears and shallow thinking to keep them from making a total commitment of their lives to this great Coach. Therefore, though they are Christians, they miss the thrilling opportunity to know how really wonderful the Master Coach is. He is, indeed, grander than they think!

Let me share with you some of the things I have come to know about this Master Coach, the matchless Christ. First, in early childhood, I came to know Christ as a wonderful person, about whom I had heard many fine things from my parents, Sunday-school teachers, ministers, and other fine Christians. Although I admired Him greatly as a person, I did not feel the sense of belonging to Him that one feels toward a loved one. Therefore, I did not know Jesus in the one way in which He most desired me to know Him.

Second, at nine, I came to know Him as Saviour. As I sat in a front pew of a church in my home town,

I listened to my pastor explain the plan of salvation. He told how Jesus gave up His place in heaven to come down to a cruel, sinful world, seeking to win individuals back to God, and that the ultimate price He paid was death on the cross. Upon realizing that Christ had died in my place for my sins, I gave my heart in faith to Him that morning. He was no longer just a wonderful person: He had become a very personal Saviour.

Now, nineteen years later, I am so glad that I did come to know Him in this all-important way. Although I had happiness in my heart on the morning of my decision, the perspective of nearly two decades helps me to realize that He saved me *from* a life of disappointment, frustration, and defeat and led me *to* a life of joy and victory. I am even more grateful to Him than I would be toward an individual who had saved me from drowning in a lake or burning in a fire. The happiness of knowing Christ as *Saviour* grows with the years!

Third, I have come to know Christ as Lord, Coach, Director of my life. In my university days, I met individuals through whose lives I learned this valuable lesson: the individual who comes to know Christ as Saviour and not as Lord of his life has missed so much of the richness of the Christian experience. Those individuals with whom I had contact on the university campus were experiencing a joy, a victory, and a usefulness which, at that time, I had not come to feel. I was a Christian; they were Christians; yet, in my life there was something missing. Finally, it dawned on me that those individuals were experiencing greater dimensions of joy, victory, and usefulness because they had permitted Christ full control of their lives in all of their considerations and relationships. Or, to put it differently, they had found that this Master Coach gave much better directions for their lives than they themselves could have devised.

I took my cue from the splendid lives of these Christ-controlled university friends: I committed my life fully to the control of the Master Coach. In these years since that commitment, I have found that Christ gives the very best instructions: therefore I am so glad that I have come to know him as *Lord of my life.*

In the Christian life we are sometimes called upon to give up some things that seem to be the most important items in our lives, but which the Lord of our lives wants to replace with something better. For example, at the age of thirteen, I began to play baseball. I played it with enthusiasm and with growing devotion. Inevitably, my one big dream for the future came to be professional baseball. That dream grew in my mind as friends added their encouragement and enthusiasm. But, between my junior and senior years in the university, the Lord of my life began to take away *my* dream and to replace it with *His* plan for my life, a process which continued for over a year, because I was reluctant to relinquish my dream of glory, glitter, and gold. Most surely, it *is* God's will for many young men to go into professional sports, but it was evidently not His will for me.

As I look back upon that experience, I am grateful that I permitted Christ's plan for my life to replace my dream, for I am playing in a league of greater significance than my dream would ever have permitted—the league of youth work—in which God permits me the indescribable joy and privilege of working with young people to prepare them to "come to bat" prepared to perform victoriously.

Therefore, young friend, if this wonderful Master Coach should call upon *you* to give up something which you hold dear, remember that He never asks His followers to *give up* something without helping them to know clearly what it is He wishes them to *take up* in its place. And one of these days in your bright future, as you look back upon your experience of giving up and taking up, you will discover that what Christ asked you to give up would never have been as wonderful for you and for others touched by your life, as the joyous thing He asked you to take up.

Fourth, in addition to coming to know Christ as a *wonderful Person,* as the *only Saviour,* and as *wise Lord* of my life, I have come to know Him in another way: I have come to know and love him as Friend, Buddy, Companion, and Pal. He wants to be to each of His followers "one who sticketh closer than a brother," One who helps us in all of life's decisions—little and large, One who wants to walk with us daily to assure us constantly that He cares, that we matter to Him, and that He wants to help.

In this joyously personal dimension of my association with Christ, I have felt Him with me on the baseball diamond as really as if my eyes could see Him. I have felt His presence in my dormitory rooms, in the classrooms, and in my car as I have traveled from campuses to other points. I knew that He understood my problems, and that He wanted to assist me in finding the wisest and happiest solutions. I feel that He is greatly interested in my hopes and ideals for marriage, and I have the happy confidence that He will guide me in this important decision.

I am happy that I have come to know Christ in all

of these wonderful ways; because, if I had missed knowing Him in any one of these ways, I would have been the loser. *What do you know of Christ from your own personal experiences?* Do you know Him in all the wonderful ways in which He can be known? The wonder of it all to me is this: the more you permit Christ to mean to you in your day-by-day living, the more wonderful He will become to you. Then, to you as to so many other members of His team, this Master Coach will come to be so much grander than you ever thought!

14

Errors—And Home Runs

(Matthew 26:69–75, Acts 2:14–41)

Peter's experiences of falling and rising again have given courage to Christians in all centuries of Christianity's history. There is no question about his mistakes: he made them more than once, including the colossal mistake (recorded in MATTHEW 26:69-75) of thrice denying Christ, despite his earlier affirmation that he would die before denying his Lord.

But his experiences include times, also, in which he scored what baseball devotees would surely classify as spine-tingling home runs. In his immortal confession, "Thou are the Christ, the Son of the living God," an affirmation which thrilled the heart of Christ and evoked a cherished blessing, and in his heroic presentation of the gospel at the Pentecostal experience in Acts 2 he scored home runs, which the annals of Christianity will cherish with the highest regard. In the latter experience, there were three thousand individuals who came to faith in Christ, largely in response to the magnificent spiritual achievement of "the man at bat."

Two aspects of Peter's errors and home runs are worthy of pointing out: *First,* He admitted his errors quickly; and, to use the descriptive language of several writers, he always "fell forward," getting up quickly to try again. He did not permit his errors to become haunting ghosts or stumbling blocks that diminished his confidence or dissuaded him from trying again. Had he done so, he could well have been numbered with the might-have-beens of history. Instead, his errors became stepping stones, which he mounted with increased wisdom to perform at a finer level.

Second, He did not permit his moments of great performance to bring either self-satisfaction or vanity to his heart. Either of those attitudes would have robbed him of the feeling that he must strive constantly to finer achievements. If he had lived on the oft-recited memory of Jesus' citation at the time of his great confession or in the dramatic recitation of that tremendous victory at Pentecost, he could well have missed the chance to become one of Christianity's immortal heroes.

In all ages, including right now, people who accomplish in any constructive field are people who have made mistakes, some of them rather large ones. As someone so sagely observed, people who don't make mistakes are either people in the cemetery or people who aren't accomplishing anything! Those who fear to try because they fear they will make mistakes are treated to the anonymity of oblivion by succeeding ages. So, since mistakes—errors in the game—are highly probable, how shall the young and ambitious player in this game of life regard them?

He will be wise to obtain the finest preparation obtainable for both life and vocation; in every area of learning and performing, the greater the wisdom, the less likelihood of mistake-making. In the area of daily living, there is no instruction to compare with the example and teaching of Jesus. Many people who have been well prepared in their vocations have fallen into tragic mistakes because of an inadequate knowledge of the teachings of Jesus or because of an inconsistent translation of those teachings into the crucible of everyday living. This knowledge of the Master-Counselor's example and teaching is a lifelong process: one needs to sit constantly at His feet to learn His way well and to achieve the motivations to pursue that way with confidence and joy.

Also, the young player in this all important game of life will want to achieve the fullest and finest training for his lifework, be that work humble or at high level. Literally a thousand and one mistakes are made daily—some by people performing very sensitive tasks—which would never have been made had the persons involved not skimmed over or taken lightly some facets of preparation in the past. If you are now a rookie or a rising star in the game, please don't settle for less than the best training available in your chosen vocation. However long it takes, however hard it may be, that best available training will pay off throughout your life in error-reduction and in the thrill of problems solved.

The aspiring young player, fortified by the best preparation for vocation and continuing preparation for living, will fix in his heart this nugget of common sense: if, despite my best preparation and performance, errors occur, I shall neither laugh them off as meaningless nor harbor them in my heart as malignancies. "I shall face them honestly and learn from them wisely." Such questions as "Why did this occur? What were my failures? What do I need to do to make sure that this does not occur again?" will bring wisdom from which will grow more accurate performance in the future.

In my years of counseling I have known young people to make serious mistakes in college or early in their careers, but they learned from those mistakes with humility and dedication and have come now to positions of trust, honor, and brilliant achievement. And there are those who have made mistakes in going against their knowledge of Christian principle and vocational integrity, mistakes which have led to public censure and, at times, to imprisonment, but they have made the long and difficult climb back to respect and achievement because they would not let mistakes pronounce a verdict of doom upon their careers. You, too, can perform in the wonderful tradition of Peter, who, having made errors that lost some innings, came back to knock home runs which won thrilling games.

HOME-RUN DEMEANOR

There is as great danger that home-run vanity will spoil the spirit of the player as that costly errors will defeat his will to win. How shall the home-run king take the glory and glamor of striking victories?

He will never forget to be grateful for and to those who have helped him become a high-level performer: the people who encouraged him in his first attempts, the people who loved him when he was unlovable, the people who helped him find his weaknesses and overcome them, the people who helped him know his strength and develop it, the people who gave him opportunities to gain experience and to develop the skills which brought him to high levels of inspiring living and skillful performance. Most of all, he will never forget God, who gave him his abilities and the Christ who has given him the power to live and to perform so as to inspire his associates and thrill the spectators in the stands. This pervasive, lifelong gratitude will cause him to be ever mindful of the suggestion that "but for the grace of God, the power of Christ, and the devotion of friends, I would not be what I am." This spirit will bring a wonderful attribute called *humility,* which, when seen in the lives of the great, is seen in its most glorious light.

He will never feel that he "has it made"; rather, he will say, as a wonderful, young and talented helper of mine said often in my presence when he was complimented, "I am grateful, but I have so far to go!" And he kept on striving constantly to do all of his work more skillfully.

I know an educator who, not satisfied with one earned doctor's degree, went abroad to an internationally known university to earn another such degree. Not satisfied with that accumulation of learning in order to teach well, he spends summers and sabbaticals in other universities for continuing study. He reads more books in the average year than a dozen of his fellow-professors combined. Despite his scintillating, incredibly rich mental resources, he still feels that he does not "have it made"—that he must keep going forward to achieve additional resources to share with his students.

I know a magnificent Christian who is so much more like Jesus than the Christians who surround him—a man of whom so many have said, "You are the most wonderful Christian I have ever known." When he hears these words, his face reflects unmistakable surprise and evident self-dissatisfaction, and he says with a humility which warms one's heart, "But I have so far to go in becoming all Christ wants me to be." His home runs, though numerous and thrilling, have never brought a sense of self satisfaction.

All of us can so well and wisely say with Paul, a home-run king if there ever was one, these significant words:

"Yet, my brothers, I do not consider myself to have 'arrived' spiritually, nor do I consider myself already perfect. But I keep going on, grasping ever more firmly that purpose for which Christ Jesus grasped me. My brothers, I do not consider myself to have fully grasped it even now. But I do concentrate on this: I leave the past behind and with hands outstretched to whatever lies ahead I go straight for the goal— my reward the honor of my high calling by God in Christ Jesus" (PHILIPPIANS 3:13-14, PHILLIPS).

A professional athlete who had won accolades and honors almost too numerous to mention was asked by an interviewer, "What do you consider to be the greatest honor you have won?" With humility and radiance, the athlete replied, "The greatest honor which has ever come to me is not an honor which I won: it is the honor conferred upon me by one named Christ, whose coming into my heart made my life what it could never have been otherwise." This awareness kept that notable athlete from vanity.

There will be both errors and home runs for you, too, young friend. Tuck the suggestions of this chapter into your heart for the times when discouragement from errors or vanity from home runs may knock at the door of your heart. Don't let either of those villains inside your heart!

Did you hear the umpire? He yelled "Batter up." It's your turn at bat. More folks than you imagine are believing in you, counting on you, loving you, and asking only that you do your best.

Suggestions for Additional Reading

Chapter 1

> *I Dare You.* William H. Danforth. Privately Printed, Twentieth Edition in 1945.
> *Living Miracles.* James C. Hefley. Zondervan Press, Grand Rapids, 1964.
> *Looking at You.* Norah Smaridge. Abingdon Press, New York and Nashville, 1962.
> *Search For Identity.* Earl Jabay. Zondervan Press, Grand Rapids, 1967.
> *The Goal and The Glory.* Ted Simonson, Ed. Fleming H. Revell, Westwood, N.J., 1962.
> *To Be Somebody.* Zan Skelton. Moody Press, Chicago, 1967.

Chapters 2 and 3

> *Careers for You.* Erma Paul Ferrari. Abingdon Press, New York and Nashville, 1953.
> *Find Out for Yourself.* Eugenia Price. Zondervan Press, Grand Rapids, 1963.
> *Your Next Big Step.* G. Kearnie Keegan. Broadman Press, Nashville, 1960.

Chapters 4 and 5

> *How To Stand Up For What You Believe.* Herbert J. Detweiler. Association Press, N.Y., 1966.
> *It's Your Turn Now.* Jack R. Noffsinger. Broadman Press, Nashville, 1964.
> *I've Been Wondering.* Fayly H. Cothern. Broadman Press, Nashville, 1956.
> *Right or Wrong?* T. B. Maston. Broadman Press, Nashville, 1955.

ADDITIONAL READING

Chapter 6

Why Am I Here? Where Am I Going? Letha Scanzoni. Fleming H. Revell, Westwood, N.J., 1966.

Chapter 7

Does Anyone Here Know God? Gladys Hunt. Zondervan Press, Grand Rapids, 1967.
Your Influence Is Showing. Leslie B. Flynn. Broadman Press, Nashville, 1967.

Chapter 8

Your Other Vocation. Elton Trueblood. Harper & Row, New York.

Chapter 9

Love and the Facts Of Life. Evelyn Millis Duvall. Association Press, New York, 1963.
Why Wait 'Till Marriage? Evelyn Millis Duvall. Association Press, New York, 1965.
Youth Considers Marriage. David R. Mace. Nelson, 1966.

Chapter 10

Dedicated Dave. Granville C. Sandusky. Exposition Press, New York, 1966.
In Spite of All. Archer Wallace. Abingdon Press, New York and Nashville, 1944.
Making the Most of What Life Brings. Theodore F. Adams. Harper & Row, New York, 1957.
Neither Down Nor Out. Chester E. Swor. Broadman Press, Nashville, 1966.

Chapter 11

A Teen-Ager's First Car. Henry Seegar Felson. Dodd, Mead & Co., New York, 1966.

ADDITIONAL READING

Ride The Wild Horses. J. Wallace Hamilton. Fleming H. Revell, Westwood, N.J., 1952.
Take A Look At Yourself. John Homer Miller. Abingdon Press, New York and Nashville, 1950.
You Can Win. Norman Vincent Peale. Garden City Publishing Company, New York, 1949.

Chapter 12

Courage to Conquer. LeRoy King, Ed. Fleming H. Revell, Westwood, N.J., 1966.
In His Steps. Charles M. Sheldon. Grossett and Dunlap, New York.
The Heart Of A Champion. Bob Richards. Fleming H. Revell, Westwood, N.J., 1959.
The Magic Of Believing. C. M. Bristol. Prentice Hall, Englewood Cliffs, N.J., 1957.

Chapter 13

A Faith For Youth. Joseph James Murray. John Knox Press, Richmond, 1948. Chapters VI, XII, XIII.
Calling Life's Signals. Steve Sloan. Zondervan Press, Grand Rapids, 1967.
Teen-Ager, Christ is for You. Walter Riess. Concordia Press, St. Louis, 1957.
What Would Jesus Do? Glenn Clark. MacAlester Park Publishing Co., St. Paul, 1950.

Chapter 14

Play Ball. James C. Hefley. Zondervan Press, Grand Rapids, 1964.
The Freedom To Fail. G. Don Gilmore, Fleming H. Revell, Westwood, N.J., 1966.